AAASO
THIS
BOOK
BELONGS
TO
AMANGANI

GRAND TETON
EXPLORERS GUIDE

CARL SCHREIER

with introduction by MARGARET E. MURIE

HOMESTEAD PUBLISHING
Moose, Wyoming

Library of Congress Catalog Card Number 96-77304
ISBN 0-943972-01-9 (paperback)
ISBN 0-943972-54-X (hardcover)
Printed in Singapore.

HOMESTEAD PUBLISHING
Box 193, Moose, Wyoming 83012

Acknowledgments
Design and geologic diagrams by Carl Schreier
Special appreciation to Eric Soyland of Grand Valley Aviation, Driggs, Idaho,
for aerial flights.

Photographic Credits
Photography and illustrations by the author, Carl Schreier, unless otherwise noted.
Other photography by: Steve Baldwin 9, 17, 31, 49; Raymond Gehman 20, 33, 42; Rick Konrad 34;
Scott McKinley 15, 26, 28, 29, 37, 38, 39.
Front Cover: The Teton Range from Schwabacher Landing.
Back cover: The Cathedral Group.
Contents page: Spring storm over Mount Teewinot.

Historical Photographic Credits for History Chapter, Pages 52–53, 55
Rockefellers: Courtesy the Schreier Collection.
Colter Stone: Photo by Harrison Crandall, Courtesy the Schreier Collection.
Hunting Scene: Photo by Sheffield, Courtesy the Schreier Collection.
Katherine Yokel Brown: Courtesy John Waldron, the Schreier Collection.
Jenny Lake Vista: Courtesy the Schreier Collection.
Canoeing String Lake, 1920s: Courtesy the Schreier Collection.

CONTENTS

❀ INTRODUCTION ❀

Whether you are a tourist, newcomer, or resident of this valley, here is your small but powerful companion to illuminate and enrich your experience of this beautiful world of the Tetons. Put your companion in your pocket or in the top of your pack—you will reach for it often, for Grand Teton National Park holds niches and enrichment beyond any casual viewing.

There are countless "things to do" in this park, all of which can be enjoyed without damage to the treasure we have here. This book will list them for you. But beyond the "doing" there is the real and legitimate thrill of *learning*. In a meadow full of flowers, reach for your companion. It will give them names. While gazing at the Tetons themselves, reach for your companion and learn how they came to be and how this valley was made.

On a trail, when a small animal sits on a rock chewing a grassblade—reach for the book—it will tell you who is chewing what and why.

If you can't stay through all the seasons, read about them. The definite four seasons are a notable and challenging and satisfying aspect of this national park.

As you travel through the park, you may wonder about its history—reach again for your companion.

Please, dear visitor, travel here with open mind and heart. Put all other concerns aside. Look, listen, smell, touch. Go gently and become immersed in a natural world. For the memories will enrich you for the rest of your days.

Margaret E. Murie
Conservationist/Writer
Moose, Wyoming

ENJOYING THE TETONS
Outdoor Activities

There is a world awaiting here in the Grand Tetons for any adventurer or explorer. But this seemingly rugged and austere range is not just reserved for the mountaineer; its scenery, seasons, wildlife, wildflowers, geology and history await exploration by all.

For the recreationist, there are limitless outdoor activities, ranging from a leisurely evening lakeshore stroll to an arduous climb up the north face of the Grand Teton. Hiking, backpacking, mountaineering, rafting, canoeing, photography, and just plain gazing are the most popular pastimes here.

Keep in mind, however, that the Tetons are more than a playground. The natural history—trees, geology, wildlife and wildflowers—makes this area unique.

To enhance the joy of a visit here, visitors need to leave the confines of an automobile to

Hiking, climbing, photography and mountain gazing represent some of the more popular ways to enjoy Grand Teton National Park.

stretch their legs on a forest trail and breathe the fresh mountain air. Take advantage when a canyon trail beckons to be hiked, or a wildflower asks to be smelled.

The Tetons and Jackson Hole are renowned for hiking and backpacking, and walking is the best way to become immersed in the environment and enjoy the area. More than 200 miles of well-maintained trails wind their ways throughout the park. The trails offer opportunities ranging from short, self-guided hikes to extended week-long backpacking trips. Each is equally enjoyable. A few of the most popular hikes are listed by area at the end of this chapter.

Backpacking is a way to explore the remote country while leaving the crowds for the solitude of the mountains. Backcountry camping is allowed in the canyons above 7,000 feet, but campsite permits are required. Be careful to protect the fragile environment of the high country so others can continue to experience solitude in popular areas.

The major backpacking route is the Teton Crest Trail. It begins in the southern end of the park and wanders along the backbone of the Teton Range to Paintbrush Canyon. Other trails lead up the major canyons to connect with the Teton Crest Trail. By hiking up a canyon and joining the Crest Trail, and then hiking down another canyon, backpackers can travel a variety of routes.

A popular overnight trip, for example, is the 19.5-mile Paintbrush Canyon to Cascade Canyon loop via Lake Solitude. A longer trip would traverse the entire length of the Teton Crest Trail, from Phillips Canyon to Paintbrush Canyon—a total of 40.2 miles.

For a more leisurely trip, the campsites along Leigh Lake are less strenuous to reach. You also can paddle to them by canoe—an ideal overnighter. The less-frequented northern section of the park also is an excellent area for backpacking. Before planning a trip, keep in mind that most high-country trails and passes usually are

snow-covered until mid-July, while the lower valley trails generally are clear by late May.

The mountains also appeal to more adventurous souls. During the warm summer months—mid-July to September—climbers from throughout the world converge here. Climbers reach the Grand Teton summit nearly every day during this time. Through strong field glasses, observers often can see climbers making their way to a mountain summit. Winter climbing recently has grown in popularity too.

Climbing is hazardous and is not recommended for the novice who lacks experience with technical climbing gear and knowledge of the mountain and its ever-changing climate. The best way to gain experience and to familiarize yourself with the terrain is to take climbing classes from experienced and authorized guides.

Climbers are not the only ones who can enjoy the peaks. The mountains are appealing from any location in the park. Floating the Snake River adds a special attraction. Whether you float with your own raft or with a commercial river guide, the river is an excellent place to see wildlife and to get a novel view of the Tetons. String Lake also is a popular and tranquil lake for canoeing with your own canoe or a rented boat. From there, with a tenth of a mile portage, you can access Leigh Lake as well.

Climbing the Grand and floating the region's rivers are just two ways to explore the ruggedness of the Tetons.

The photographic possibilities in the park also are limitless. The best way to be ready for that once-in-a-lifetime shot is to keep your camera with you constantly. Whether you are hiking or canoeing, wildlife is unpredictable. If you keep your camera ready, you may be able to capture some rare moments.

The best area to photograph moose, swans, otters, and bison is at the Oxbow Bend of the Snake River, between Moran and the Jackson Lake Dam. Early mornings and evenings are the best times to see wildlife. At those times, animals are more active than during midday, when they avoid heat and insects. The drive up to Signal Mountain Summit—considered the premier viewpoint for Jackson Lake and Teton sunsets—is rewarding, especially in the evening.

HIKING TRAILS IN THE COLTER BAY & JACKSON LAKE LODGE AREA

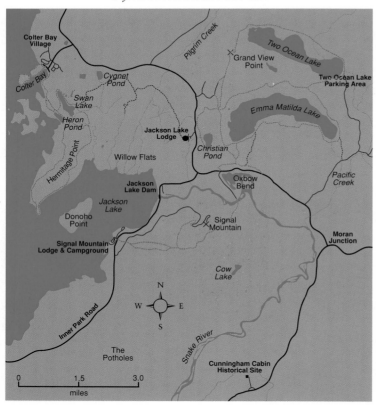

Colter Bay and Jackson Lake Lodge offer a number of good hikes, which originate from the campground area or lodge. This is considered the best locale for wildlife viewing, and all trails provide scenic vistas.

COLTER BAY NATURE TRAIL
Length: 1.7-mile loop.

This easygoing trail begins just behind the Colter Bay Visitor Center.

The trail follows the Colter Bay Shore and crosses a bridge to a small island, then loops around the island along the Jackson Lake shoreline back to the visitor center. This recommended short evening hike provides a superb view of sunsets behind Mount Moran and Jackson Lake.

CHRISTIAN POND TRAIL
Length: 3.2-mile loop from the road at Christian Creek Bridge.

This is a good hike leading east from Jackson Lake Lodge and traversing excellent habitat for wildlife viewing. Early mornings often will reward hikers with swan, coyote and moose sightings. The undulating trail circumvents a small pond through a variety of habitats, including willow, sagebrush, marsh, and lodgepole-pine forest.

GRAND VIEW POINT TRAIL
Length: 1.1 miles, one way (3 miles from Jackson Lake Lodge).

This hike provides an overview of the Teton Range, Jackson Lake, and Two Ocean and Emma Matilda lakes. It can be accessed by Jackson Lake Lodge, via Christian Pond, or by driving to the trailhead 0.9 miles north of the Jackson Lake Lodge intersection, then following a dirt road for a half mile to the start.

EMMA MATILDA AND TWO OCEAN LAKES TRAIL
Lengths: Emma Matilda Lake Trail from:
Jackson Lake Lodge: 10.1-mile loop.
Two Ocean Lake parking area: 10-mile loop.
Two Ocean Lake Trail from:
Jackson Lake Lodge: 11.6-mile loop.
Two Ocean Lake parking area: 8.5-mile loop.
For a long day-hike, the Emma Matilda and Two Ocean Lakes Trail

The Colter Bay region has a varied landscape, with Mount Moran rising from Jackson Lake.

is recommended. Depending upon your time and desire, you can link a number of trails to make either a short hike or a longer one that visits both lakes and Grand View Point. Both lakes can be reached from either Jackson Lake Lodge on the west side, or by driving up Pacific Creek on the east side to Two Ocean Lake parking area and trailhead.

SWAN LAKE
AND HERON POND TRAIL
Length: 2.5-mile loop.

No other trail is better than the Swan Lake and Heron Pond Trail for an early-morning hike. To find the trailhead, follow the paved road south from the Colter Bay Visitor Center past the marina to the end of the parking area. From there the trail heads into the lodgepole forest. Old roads and trails to sewage ponds, maintenance sheds and other access areas are confusing; use

Mount Moran, left, dominates the landscape from many of the Colter Bay trails. Early morning hikes will reward most hikers with misty mountains and candid views of wildlife.

In a more remote region of the Colter Bay area, above, along the Continental Divide, a small creek straddles the Divide before splitting into two separate creeks, flowing in opposite direcitons to the Pacific and Atlantic oceans.

your sense of direction to find the proper route. A loop trail will take you past an abandoned sewage settling pond and then on to Swan Lake and Heron Pond. During early morning, swans, beaver, moose, and an abundance of bird life usually are found there. It is also an

excellent trail for forest wildflowers.

HERMITAGE POINT TRAIL
Length: 9.1-mile loop.

If you have done the Swan Lake Trail as an early-morning hike, this is a good trail to continue on for an afternoon hike. The trailhead is the same as Swan Lake Trail. After skirting Swan Lake and Heron Pond, the trail loops south around the tip of a peninsula and wanders through lodgepole pine and sagebrush meadow

openings and lake-shore vistas. But, like the beginning of Swan Lake, there are numerous unmarked trails in this area, and finding the correct trail often can be frustrating. Keep a good sense of where you are by monitoring landmarks.

SIGNAL MOUNTAIN TRAIL
Length: 3 miles, one way.

This 3-mile trail to the summit of Signal Mountain begins at the entrance to Signal Mountain Campground. Walk down the "Boat Launch" road for about 200 yards. From there, a trail leaves the road and leads east into the lodgepole pines and cuts across the highway. After two-tenths of a mile, it crosses the Signal Mountain Road, past Moose Pond, and then divides into a north Ridge Trail and a south Lake Trail. Both merge again after a mile and continue up a small gully and a large switchback 1.5 miles to Jackson Lake Overlook near the actual summit of Signal Mountain. From there, the summit is accessible by following the road.

HIKING TRAILS IN THE JENNY LAKE & STRING LAKE AREA

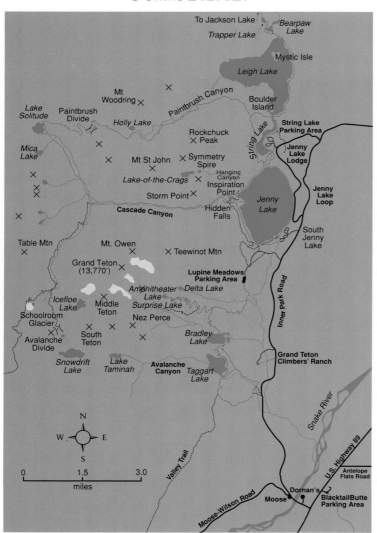

Jenny Lake is known as the crossroads for hiking and climbing in Grand Teton, and most of the major trailheads originate here. Trails provide relatively easy accessibility into the mountains to waterfalls, quiet lakes, glaciers and scenic vistas.

JENNY LAKE TRAIL
Length: 6.5-mile loop

Jenny Lake was named after the Indian wife of Beaver Dick Leigh (Leigh Lake), who was a trapper and guide during the 1870s. The trail around the lake is easygoing and starts at the Jenny Lake or String Lake parking area. This trail is most enjoyable in the morning or evening, when it is cooler and fewer people are around. The drawback is that the trail parallels, or in some cases adjoins, the road on the east side.

HIDDEN FALLS AND INSPIRATION POINT TRAIL
Lengths: Hidden Falls from:

Jenny Lake West Shore Boat Dock: 0.5 miles, one way.

Jenny Lake Ranger Station: 2.3 miles, one way.

Inspiration Point from:

Jenny Lake West Shore Boat Dock: 1 mile, one way.

Jenny Lake Ranger Station: 2.8 miles, one way.

There are two ways to reach Hidden Falls and Inspiration Point. The first is to hike from the Jenny Lake parking area along the southern shore of the lake and follow Cascade Creek to the falls. The other is to take the shuttle boat (for a fee) from the east to west shore of the lake, reducing the hiking distance by 2 miles. The East Shore Boat Dock is 300 yards east of the parking area at the outlet of Jenny Lake. To reach Inspiration Point from the West Shore Boat Dock, continue a half mile past Hidden Falls to an overlook at 6,200 feet with an excellent view of Jenny Lake, Jackson Hole, and the mouth of Cascade Canyon.

View from Lake Solitude on the Cascade Canyon Trail.

CASCADE CANYON
AND LAKE SOLITUDE TRAIL

Lengths: Lake Solitude from:

    Jenny Lake Boat Dock: 8.6 miles, one way.

    Jenny Lake West Shore Boat Dock: 6.9 miles, one way.

    String Lake parking area: 8.4 miles, one way.

    To reach Lake Solitude, follow the trail to Hidden Falls and Inspiration Point. The trail continues up Cascade Canyon for 3.6 miles to its forks. The north fork leads to Lake Solitude, at an elevation of 9,035 feet. The canyon has a unique glacial history. Scoured walls and a broad U-shaped valley are clues to its past, and this evidence is visible during your hike through the canyon. Lake Solitude is a small tarn located in a cirque, but the view to the southeast, down the valley, provides a unique aspect of the Grand Teton.

AMPHITHEATER
AND SURPRISE LAKES TRAIL

Length: 4.8 miles, one way.

    This is an excellent opportunity to reach treeline in a short hike. It is a strenuous hike, with an elevation gain of nearly 3,000 feet in 4 miles, but the view of the valley and changes in habitat

Hiking and photography—the two most popular ways to explore here—go hand-in-hand in Grand Teton National Park. The hike to Hidden Falls, left, and a reflective moment along String Lake, right, both offer memorable experiences.

and vegetation along the way provide relief. The trail begins at Lupine Meadows parking area, just south of Jenny Lake.

STRING LAKE TRAILS

Lengths: String Lake parking area to:

Leigh Lake outlet: 0.9 miles, one way.

Trail around String Lake: 3.5-mile loop.

Holly Lake: 6.2 miles, one way.

The String Lake trails are good for afternoon hikes in July and August, when the mountain lakes have warmed enough for swimming. The trailhead begins at the north end of the String Lake parking area. From there, the path leads to the outlet of Leigh Lake, where it turns west at a junction crossing a bridge. Eventually, it leads west up Paintbrush Canyon to Holly Lake. But for those who want to continue a leisurely hike around String Lake, the trail splits a half mile west of the bridge and leads back to the parking area, or joins the Jenny Lake Trail.

BRADLEY AND TAGGART LAKES TRAIL

Lengths: Bradley and Taggart Lake parking area to:

Bradley Lake: 1.6 miles, one way.

Taggart Lake: 2 miles, one way.

The trailhead is about 2 miles north of Moose on the Teton Park Road. The trail wanders through sagebrush meadows and lodgepole stands as it leads to Taggart and Bradley lakes. The trails are well-marked, and there is a shortcut for the return to the parking area.

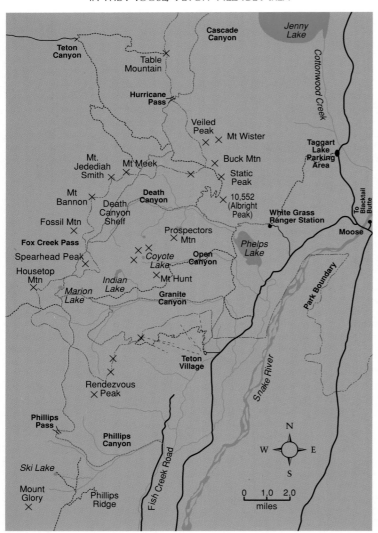

HIKING TRAILS
IN THE MOOSE/TETON VILLAGE AREA

The Moose area has a number of short, easygoing day hikes leading to glacier-formed lakes and canyons. This area also has longer trails that lead through canyon meadows colored by wildflowers.

PHELPS LAKE AND DEATH CANYON TRAIL

Lengths: Whitegrass Ranger Station to:

Phelps Lake Overlook: 0.9 miles, one way.

Phelps Lake: 2 miles, one way.

Death Canyon Ranger Station: 3.7 miles, one way.

The trail starts at the Whitegrass Ranger Station south of Moose. To get there, take the Moose-Wilson Road, across from the Moose Visitor Center. Follow the road 3.1 miles to signs at a junction and drive to the ranger station. There, the trail starts and will lead to the Phelps Lake Overlook—an overgrown glacial moraine that provides a spectacular view. The trail continues down the moraine to Phelps Lake and Death Canyon. A hike up the canyon is rewarding, and it is just as interesting geologically as is Cascade Canyon. During early July, this is perhaps one of the best canyons for wildflowers, and it also is noted for its abundant wildlife.

GRANITE CANYON TRAIL

Lengths: Granite Canyon Trail parking area to:

Granite Canyon Junction and Ranger Station: 1.6 miles, one way.

Rendezvous Mountain Trail Junction: 6.3 miles, one way.

Marion Lake: 8.8 miles, one way.

Rendezvous Mountain (Aerial Tram): 11.5 miles, one way.

Granite Canyon parking area is 6 miles south of Moose on the Moose-Wilson Road. Hiking this trail system can be strenuous and is recommended principally for active people. The trail to Granite Canyon Junction leads through sagebrush meadows and aspen groves before

The short hike to the Phelps Lake Overlook, an overgrown glacial moraine, is an opportunity to observe the geology, wildlife, and wildflowers for which Grand Teton National Park is famous.

reaching the mouth of Granite Canyon. The trail is gentle until the Rendezvous Trail Junction, and from there to Marion Lake or Rendezvous Mountain, it becomes steeper. The easiest way to do the Rendezvous Mountain trip is to ride the aerial tram (for a fee) from Teton Village and then hike down the trail to the Granite Trail parking area or return to Teton Village via the Valley Trail along the base of the Teton Range.

BLACKTAIL BUTTE
Length: 2.3 miles, one way.

Blacktail Butte is a geological anomaly in the middle of Jackson Hole. Glaciers, dating 15,000 to 250,000 years ago, filled and flowed down the valley, overriding Blacktail Butte. The large continental ice sheets polished and formed the Madison limestone as the ice flowed over and around the butte, sculpting it into its present boat-shaped form.

Trail access to the butte is located on the northwest corner, 0.9 miles north of Moose

An extended trip along the Teton Crest Trail into the backcountry of Alaska Basin, left, provides hikers with incredible vistas and remarkable shows of wildflowers. Indian paintbrush, right, above, and other colorful flowers fill the large basin during July and August, when flowers at lower elevations have already faded.

Junction and just off the highway. A parking area is provided at the base of the vertical limestone wall. This wall is a popular learning and practice rock for climbers. Twenty or more relatively difficult routes test top-roped climbers on the 5.9 to 5.12c classed climbs.

Just south of the wall is a trail and staircase that provide top roping access for climbs. This trail also leads to the top of Blacktail Butte (7,688 feet), after a strenuous 1,150-foot gain. From the top is an excellent view of the Teton Range and the surrounding Jackson Hole.

Another hike from the parking area skirts the western base of the butte. The trail leads directly south from the parking area and follows an old road and irrigation ditch. This trail leads to several isolated ravines. Some have springs, and the ravines

are surprisingly cool and moist with lush vegetation and the perfect hideaway on a hot summer day. The trail continues to the southern end of the butte, still skirting its edge, and eventually joins the Gros Ventre-Kelly road near the campground.

Trails to the summit of the butte also are accessible from the southern end. These are longer but not as steep.

❦ SEASONS ❦
The Four Changes

The seasons of Grand Teton are distinct and extreme, but they define and characterize the mountain mystique. Each season brings with it a unique change in scenery, temperature, and wildlife. By following the seasons, it is possible to become acquainted with the moods of the mountains themselves.

SPRING

When spring arrives in Jackson Hole, there is a special fresh quality to the air. Winter has passed, and each successive day brings warmth and new life.

Spring begins in the Tetons when most other areas are claiming summer. Late spring snowstorms and chilly mornings are reminders of

A spring morning along the Snake River at Schwabacher Landing provides the best opportunities to observe the rapidly changing season.

winter's last hold. By the middle of April, the snowpack begins to melt, until the first spring flowers are able to push their way through. Bright yellow buttercups are the first true signs of this season. But they actually started growing during the previous fall, developing the first signs of flower buds and leaves. The darkness of winter, and the extreme cold, kept them dormant but with the increasing daylight of spring, they resume their growth, pushing through the snow crust. Soon afterward, yellowbells, pasqueflowers, spring beauties, shooting stars and steer's heads follow.

This also is the time of renewal for wildlife. The lean survivors of winter now have a bounty as they graze on the greening hillsides. Their bellies begin to extend, the old winter coat is replaced, and on bull elk and moose, velvet knobs begin to grow where their antlers were shed in March. Elk, moose, and bison drop their calves almost simultaneously in the lush green meadows. After the young gain strength and lose their wob-

bly legs, they follow their mothers' heels as they move to higher summer pastures with the retreating snowline.

Other animals are awakening to spring. The Uinta ground squirrel, coming out of hibernation, unplugs the entrance to its burrow and tunnels through the remaining snow to surface in sunshine. But the awakening adults, still droggy and slow from their winter's sleep and a dark object on white snow, become victim to spring's early predators. The young were born hairless, with eyes closed, during the last part of winter. They are helpless in this condition, but they will not venture out above ground on their wobbly legs until June, the beginning of summer.

Courtship is another true sign of spring. Male snipes perform their aerial acrobatics, flying zigzags in the evening sky over the National Elk Refuge. Special feathers on their wing-tips produce a hollow, tropical sound during steep dives. Male sagegrouse gather on traditional display grounds, called leks, to strut with their neck

feathers raised and wings and tails spread. Canada geese bob their heads on long, slender necks to attract attention. The air is filled with the enchanting songs of robins, meadowlarks, and red-wing blackbirds, for the benefit and attraction of a potential mate.

When the vigorous activities of courting are over, nest construction begins. For a bald eagle, osprey or swan, the task is easier because these species return to the same nest year after year. Only minor annual additions or repairs are needed. The hairy woodpecker, though, excavates a new cavity each year into an aspen, while the chickadee uses the woodpecker's abandoned hole from the year before. The barn swallow will collect mud along the banks of the Snake River and mix this with saliva to make a cement-like case under the eaves of buildings or the abutments of bridges. White trumpeter swans construct large stick and grass nests on small islands with distant unobstructed views.

Common yellowthroat and yellow warblers weave small, intricate nests of grass and leaves in willow and silverberry bushes along the banks of the Snake River. If the parents leave the nest unattended to search for food, the brown-headed cowbird may parasitize the nest. The cowbird will push the warblers eggs out of the nest and leave

her own to be adopted by the warblers. By summer, the unsuspecting mother warbler soon may be feeding young that are five times her size.

These are activities of spring. It is a busy time as animals prepare for the coming short summer.

Grand Teton is alive with the activities of spring. Nesting birds, like the trumpeter swan, left, sit patiently for a month incubating their eggs as the snowline on the Teton Range, right, progressively moves up the mountainside.

SUMMER

Spring merges into summer very quickly. Of the four seasons, these are the two with the least obvious transition. The rains of May leave the hillsides green and splotched with the color of June flowers. The brilliant yellows of arrowleaf balsamroot, biscuitroot, and sulphurflower line the roadways. As June progresses, the blues of lupines, larkspurs, and bluebells also emerge. By the fourth of July, the reds of scarlet gilia and monkey flower mark the end of the floral display. Even when the June display is over, new flowers continue to bloom and fade throughout the summer. The July visitor who missed this display in the valley can follow the retreating snowline uphill and find flowers blooming on the mountain slopes of Alaska Basin and other high-mountain meadows.

Wildlife is not as highly visible now as it was during spring. Most birds have reared their families. Even mallards and robins who raised two sets of fledglings are not as common. But other animals have moved to higher summer pastures. Elk and moose no longer are as abundant on the valley floor. Elk spend their summers in the high Teton Wilderness north of the

park, while moose seek the green riparian meadows of the mountain canyons.

But once these animals have moved from out of the valley floor, they are replaced with others that have migrated from the plains to Jackson Hole. One such animal is the prong-

horn antelope, which migrates across the Gros Ventre Mountains to spend summer on the elk and moose winter range.

By mid-July, the days become hot by Jackson Hole standards, but the evenings are pleasantly cool. Shorts, T-shirts and hiking shoes are suitable and usual attire. The retreating snowline on the mountains now is high enough and dry enough to allow backpacking. Also, camping, bicycling, canoeing, and hiking now can be done without thoughts of winter parkas.

Summer is the busiest season for everyone, wildlife and people included, and routines soon become set. Whether it is a squirrel caching pine cones for the winter or a motorist driving down a tree-lined highway, both have a tendency to overlook the obvious. Take in the scenery, the sunshine and enjoy it while you can, for it passes quickly.

As summer continues, grasses and sedges begin to cure and turn brown, and the earth and air become drier. During dry summers, dry heat or forked lightning—lightning without rain—can start forest fires.

In Grand Teton National Park, the forest is comprised of nearly 70 percent lodgepole pine, a tall narrow tree that grows in dense stands. Indians once used the slender poles for their tepees, hence its name. Lodgepole pine is a fire species, and it has adapted to that seemingly destructive force. As periodic fire passes along the ground of a lodgepole pine forest, it cleans the undergrowth and downfall and removes older trees, which, because of their age, became infected by harmful insects. Long after the fire passes, reflected heat from the scorched and blackened ground is enough to open dormant resin-sealed pine cones. The cone scales slowly open and drop seeds among the ashes. Thus as many as 100,000 seedlings will

sprout on one acre of burned forest. Each seedling will compete against the others, but only a few will survive and reach maturity in about 140 years.

If there is one event that marks the end of summer, it is the disappearance of the Uinta ground squirrel. All summer long, the ground squirrel grazes on grass and feeds upon seeds until it becomes so plump it can barely fit into its burrow. Sensing decreasing amounts of daylight, it begins to disappear underground about August 15, emerging for a few hours a day until Labor Day, when it plugs the entrance to its burrow and disappears completely.

Uinta ground squirrels, left, are active all summer, until they begin hibernation in about mid August.

During dry summers, lightning or manmade fires can start in a forest. Forest fires, right, generally do not burn everything in their paths. A mosaic of burned and unburned areas are left in their wake. The trees in Grand Teton National Park have adapted to fire by developing either a thick insulating cork-like bark or cones ready to open and release their seeds after the fire has passed. Just the smoke produced from a fire acts as a natural insecticide in reducing harmful forest pests like the pine bark beetle.

FALL

Labor Day marks the traditional beginning of fall, at least on human calendars. It is the favorite season for many. Indian summers with hot sizzling days and frigid cold nights are trademarks of this season. Deciduous trees usually do not turn color until the middle or end of September, but shrubs begin to show their autumn colors much earlier. Rose, mountain ash, and huckleberries turn brilliant red and orange, and when cottonwoods and aspen show their yellows, the show is complete.

Amidst the splendor of these fall colors begins the rutting season of elk and moose. Bull elk and moose both sport full antler racks. In the cool evenings of late September and early October, elk begin their bugling to attract cows to form harems. Each bull elk tries to outdo his competitor, and when bugling does not work to keep others away, clashes with sharp antlers will.

But most animals are preparing for winter in other ways, as the snowline begins to descend the mountainside. These animals have one of three choices—migration, adaptation or death before the onset of winter. Most birds will migrate out of the valley to warmer climates, and those that remain will at least leave the high country for a milder environment in the valley.

For a predator, the changing season means less prey than the surplus during spring and summer. The weasel adapts to the coming winter by

changing the color of its pelage, or coat, with the season to give him an added advantage. The brown summer coat is slowly shed for a pure white coat (except for the black-tipped tail), which will camouflage him in the snow. The pika, beaver, and squirrel have prepared for winter by

caching food for the long, cold months. While Uinta ground squirrels have stored body fat to carry them through their winter hibernation, other animals have little care about the oncoming cold. Grasshoppers leave their eggs in the ground to ensure a new generation; their own lives pass with the first heavy frost.

Fall also is a time of solitude. With the end of a busy summer, the tranquil serenity of a trail, broken only by the occasional chattering of a red squirrel, or the vista of a still mountain lake, or the shortening days prepare humans for the coming of a long, harsh winter.

Fall is the season for color. Aspens and cottonwoods change to golds, yellows and oranges in late September.

WINTER

Signs of winter are in the air when snow flurries begin in October, but winter does not really settle in until snow remains on the ground, usually just after Thanksgiving. One can keep track of the encroaching winter by watching the snowline advance down the mountains.

When the snow arrives, snowshoes and cross-country skis are brought out of hibernation and another world is waiting to be explored. The annual snowfall of 200 inches is enough to shroud the valley with a blanket of white. The lakes freeze over, forming large white fields. Trees are draped with snow, producing "ghosts" of unusual form. Summer trails are buried under six feet of snow. This is what becomes of the lush green valley six months after summer. A clean world, a cold world, and a white world.

Much of the busy summer activity ceases during winter. Animals try to conserve their energy to survive the cold months, and humans, too, have migrated to warmer climes or spend more time indoors near the woodstove.

A summer visitor who returns now will wonder what has happened to the once-abundant animal life. It is still around but is not as active. The Uinta ground squirrel, which stood by the trail whistling if an intruder came too close, now is six feet below the snow surface and another four feet underground curled up in hibernation. The red squirrel also is in a winter stupor, nestled among the needles in a tree cavity. Unlike the Uinta ground squirrel, the red squirrel will become restless and hungry on sunny winter days and visit his cache of pine cones. Butterflies and moths are dormant in cocoons beneath the bark of a lodgepole pine, while hairy and downy woodpeckers spend their winter in search of them. All of this life surrounds the skier who is only aware of the *chick-a-dee-dee-dee* call of the chickadee and *cawing* call of the raven.

Moose are common individually or in small family groups along the Snake River and other open streams during winter, while elk bunch to form herds at the National Elk Refuge, where the deep snow drives them from their high summer pastures.

Temperatures can drop to 40 below, with the coldest temperatures usually between Christmas and New Year's. But the skies seldom are overcast, as sunny days are common. Winter, though, is never a time to be unprepared. Always expect the worst of weather and dress accordingly, with extra warm winter clothes for outdoor activities.

While wildlife have become adapted to the cold, harsh winters of Jackson Hole, the early pioneers such as "Beaver Dick" Leigh, his Shoshone wife, Jenny, and their six children found winters to be inhospitable and unforgiving. "Beaver Dick" Leigh was an early trapper and guide in this region during the mid to late 1800s. In those early years before settlement, there were no doctors or neighbors nor help for miles around, and when a crisis arose, winter weather only made the situation worse. The realities of winter were especially brought forth during the winter of 1876 when a young Indian woman, widowed by the suicide of her husband, pregnant and with a three-year-old child, sought help from the Leigh family. But she unknowingly brought tragedy to their family during that Christmas. In a letter to his friend, Dr. Josiah Curtis—the 1872 Hayden Survey's surgeon and microscopist—"Beaver Dick" tells the sad tale of winter survival.

...we went and examined the woman and could see nothing suspisus about hur and come to the concluson that she died in child bed i asked my wife to take the little indan girle to the house and wash and clene it she sade not to do it something told hur that the child wold die but at my request she took it to the house and clened it up it played with my childron for 4 days as lively as could be and that night it broke out all over with little red spots we thought it was a rash from being washed and cept in a warme house as the child ad a cold at the time.... on the 14th my famley all feling and looking wel only my wife she complaned of drowesenes.... dick (Junior, and I) went hunting the next morning... we... run some deer out and i kiled one of them while i was dresing it i looked a crost the creek and saw some one with tom (Laverings, a friend)... thay... told me that thare was something rong at home i started for the cabin... Dick sade his mother had a bad head

Winter is shrouded in crystalline beauty, but it is also a harsh season for wildlife and people alike. Temperatures can plummet to minus 60 degrees Fahrenheit in the valley, with the week between Christmas and the New Year generally registering the coldest temperatures. The Grand Teton, right, even creates its own winter storms.

ake and wanted me at home.... my wife was seting on the flore by the stove and my youngest daughter with her.... my oldest daughter was in bed complaining with a pane in hur back and bely hur looks when she answered my questions struck my hart cold William('s) legs wekened 2 hours before i got home and he was in bed... Jonhs legs gave way and i put him to Bed tom and me was taken the same day... we did not sleep mutch we were burning up aperutly some time and chiley.... we ad both lost our apitets.... nex day about 4 o clock my wife gave birth to a child she ad broken out all over with small red spots but after the birth of the child thay all went back on hur i knew what the desise was (smallpox) as soone as i came in to the house althoe i ad never seene it before... she sleped... al night in the morning my wife sade she wanted to get up and set by the stove... she

in the house and bed and tom went over to get Mr. Anes while Tom and Anes was sounding the ice to see if a horse could cross my wife was struck with Death she rased up and looked at me streaght in the face then she got exited and cursed Mr. Anes for bringing the Indan woman back to us and she

fanted she shook all over and made rumbling noyse when she came to she sade to me what is the matter dady i told hur she had fanted from wekins... i was satisfide that hur hours was numbered and i spoke in corigenly to hur but my hart was ded within me.... it was hard work for me to answer hur without betraying my feelings but i did so the children ad got quite and some of them aslpe and i told my wife i wold go out and set fire to a brush pile to signal for tom and dick to come home.... tom drove up with Dick taken with the small pox.... i got Dick

sade she was going to die and all our children wold die and maby i wold die... she then layed downe and smiled at me... and at hur request... covered hur with blankits.... she was layeng very quite now for about 2 hours when she asked for a drink of water... and 10 minutes more she ded. Dick turned over in bed when he hurd the words and sade god bles my poore mother he then sade to me father maby we will all die.... we raped (wrapped) my wife up in a blankit and Boflo robe and put hur in the waggon bed the next morning Mr. Anes started to the resirvation

for the doctor on information how to treet the desise.... tom was getting very low downe... i knew i must ave sleep but could not get it wile layeng down.... i got up and adminestrad to my famley agane with the detirmation of doing all i could until i died.... i saw the spots go black on William and Ann Jane.... this night about 10 o clock i ad to lay downe exosted.... i felt some sines of sleep but with the sines came a heavy sweting and burning and tremors... when it left me i told tom and Anes were everything was that they might want and asked them to save some of my famley if it was posable and turned over to die i can not wright one hundredth part that passed thrue my mind at this time as i thought deth was on me/i sade Jinny i will sone be with you and fell a sleep.... whe(n) i woke up... the spots ad gone back on Dick my detirmation was to stand by them

die with them this was cristmas eve Ann Jane died about 8 o clock about the time every year i used to give them a candy puling and they mechoned about the candy puling many times while sick espechely my son John William died on the 25.... John and Elizabeth was doing well they was ahead of the rest in the desise the scale was out and drying up on the night of the 26ᵗʰ i changed watching with Anes i let Anes sleep.... tom was taken with dyaria 2 days ago and was to weak to get up to assist us enymore on the 26ᵗʰ Dick Juner died.... last night when i woke up *the fire was out but some small coles the lamp burned down and the dore of the cabin partly open i was fresing aperntly when i woke up and saw Anes lening back agenst the walle asleep it gave me a starte that i can not discribe i wok him up then got up myself my son John had comenced to swell agane... on the 27 in the morning he died on the night of the 27 i woke up cold agene and found Anes lening aganst the bed fast asleep agane... i got up as quick as my strength wold let me and woke him up but it was too late Elizabeth was over all danger by this and she caught cold and sweled up agane and died on the 28 Dec.... this was the hardist blowe of all.... me and tom layed betwixt life and death for several days... nothing else to do... when all my famely was all ded and bured....*

"Beaver Dick" Leigh survived the smallpox epidemic and, at 50, married a 14-year-old Bannock girl, Sue Tadpole. Leigh was a friend of her parents and even assisted at her birth. "Beaver Dick" died in 1899 and Sue in 1927; they had three children. "Beaver Dick" Leigh's is a tragic but common story for pioneer families. Even today, residents become snowbound and trapped by fierce winter storms. By mid-April, though, everyone greets longer daylight hours and watches the snowline recede. A new season is beginning and with it new life and a new year.

Although winter can be harsh, a nighttime snowfall, left, drapes trees in a blanket of snow, and the Snake River Overlook, right, provides the perfect vista on a winter day.

❦ WILDLIFE ❦
A Land Of Plenty

Grand Teton National Park is renowned for its abundant and varied wildlife. The surrounding area, including Yellowstone National Park, wildlife refuges, forest and wilderness areas, provide an expansive haven for the protection of wildlife and their habitat. And how does one define wildlife? It is not only the bear, moose, and elk, but includes the Western tanager, the lodgepole pine, the Indian paintbrush, the cutthroat trout, as well as the grasshopper, too. But the mega fauna—those that are described as the large, robust and showy mammals—are what attract visitors from throughout the world.

THE MAMMALS

Elk—also called wapiti by the Shawnee Indians, in reference to their light-colored rump patch—stand up to five feet tall at the shoul-

Moose are awkward-looking but their long legs are adapted to wading through marshes and streams.

ders and weigh as much as 1,000 pounds. They are, perhaps, the mammal that is most closely associated with Grand Teton. Today, the elk herd is one of the largest in North America, comprising between 7,500 and 9,000 animals.

Traditionally, elk migrated with the seasons. During spring and early summer, they gradually moved to higher summer pastures following the snowmelt to take advantage of the lush and greening forage. As fall and early winter snows drove them down to lower elevations, they gradually followed valleys and river drainages to mild open plains. During their leisurely migration to and from high summer meadows, they never lingered long enough to overuse the range and eat themselves out of house and home. But, beginning in the 1880s when human settlement increased and the town of Jackson was built on their primary migration route, their habit changed forever. Farmers and ranchers soon had almost 25,000 elk descend upon their haystacks and hay meadows every winter. This and several severe

winters, especially the winters of 1887, 1897 and 1908, led to starving and dying elk. Elk died by the thousands. This prompted concerned citizens to begin the process of feeding retained elk. Beginning in 1890, public outcry—both local and national—led the state, the U.S. Biological Survey, Congress and, in 1925, the Izzac Walton League to purchase land, eventually establishing what now is the National Elk Refuge. Today, the elk herd winters on the elk refuge north of Jackson and is fed primarily condensed alfalfa in the form of pellets; it no longer can return to its ancient wintering grounds farther south on the open plains.

Fall is the season for observing elk. Mature bulls with massive antler racks expend their reserve energy during the rutting season, bugling to attract and keep their harems of cow elk. It is one of the thrilling experiences of a Grand Teton autumn, especially during late September and October, to listen for bugling elk in the Signal Mountain or Timbered Island areas on a cool, crisp evening or morning.

Moose, the largest member of the deer family, also is the most awkward and ungainly looking. Their looks are deceiving, however, for they can walk through marshy areas or deep snow with amazing agility. They, too, sport massive antlers with flat palmate shapes, which weigh as much as 35 pounds. Moose are common residents along the Snake River during autumn, winter and spring, but by summer they move up into the cooler canyons of the Teton Range. They often take up summer residence in Cascade Canyon and, in winter, often are found in the willow flats near the Oxbow Bend of the Snake River.

Mule deer are common winter inhabitants of the valley but often migrate to the upper canyons and the high meadows of the mountains. During fall and winter, however, they usually are more common on the eastern side of the Snake River.

Pronghorn antelope, North America's fastest mammal, usually are only seasonal valley residents. They migrate across the Gros Ventre Mountains to spend the summer in the sagebrush flats. But as winter approaches, heavy snowfall is far too deep for this short-legged animal, and its choices are either to migrate east across the Gros Ventre range to the

open plains or become a victim of the harsh Jackson Hole winter.

A resident herd of *bison* wanders through the park as well. The bison are a remnant of a wildlife exhibit once located near the Oxbow of the Snake River, and later were set free. Since then, they have increased in number and, in recent years, have become a dominant animal in Grand Teton. Bison, called buffalo by early pioneers, have massive back humps and neck muscles, giving their forequarters a nearly unbalanced appearance. But this large build is useful in winter when their heads and necks move deep snow in search of buried grazing. During summer, they can be found in the Signal Mountain and Potholes area, and in early summer (May-June), their reddish colored calves can be seen frolicking in the green grass. By winter, they wander toward Kelly Warm Springs and the National Elk Refuge.

Black bears, ranging in color from brown to black to cinnamon, occasionally are seen along the canyon trails. They are not common but, when least expected, will wander through a campground in search of a meal. Follow common sense, and stash your food properly to avoid encounters with bears.

Grizzly bears are extremely rare in Grand Teton; usually, the only sightings are footprints in the northern region of the park. Grizzlies try to avoid all human contact, so they are very secretive and elusive.

Many visitors' favorite animal is the *beaver,* a water-dwelling mammal suited for the cold ponds and streams. The beaver is a nocturnal mammal who works on dams and lodges under the protection of darkness. Beaver that live in streams do not construct dams or lodges, but live in the banks with their burrow entrance below

Mule deer, left, earn their name from huge ears that are two-thirds the length of their head. Like other mountain wildlife, mule deer spend their winters in the less-harsh environment of the valley floor and migrate to higher summer pastures in the Teton Range.

Goldeneye ducklings, right, ply the waters in early spring and summer.

waterline. Blacktail Ponds, north of Moose, is the best area to find beaver in the late evening or early morning.

Coyotes often serenade summer campers to sleep. The coyote is chiefly a nocturnal animal, but it can be spotted during the day as it crosses the road and disappears in the sagebrush.

The Tetons also are an ornithologist's haven. *Trumpeter swans,* brought almost to extinction during the 1930s, nest in ponds around the Colter Bay area. The bright yellow, red and black of the *Western tanager* is a colorful summertime sight in the String Lake area. The shorelines of lakes and streams are abundant with plovers, sandpipers, common mergansers and other ducks, geese, and white pelicans. *Osprey* circle overhead waiting to dive for cutthroat trout, while bald eagles, red-tailed hawks, ravens, and falcons soar endlessly in the thermals.

The coyote, left, is an integral part of the wildlife community. Coyotes range widely, will eat almost anything, and often can be seen stalking small mammals among grazing elk, right, in the grassland-sagebrush community.

THE PLANTS

Plants constitute the other half of Teton life. Over a thousand different species of trees, shrubs, grasses, sedges, forbs and wildflowers are indigenous to the valley and mountains. But throughout the summer, wildflowers bloom and fade in colorful displays. The highlight of the wild-flower season is the third to fourth week of June. During this time, the valley's meadows are alive with the colors of the rainbow. Yellow, sunflower-like arrowleaf balsamroots are in full bloom, bright red Indian paintbrush and the blue pealike lupines each add their contrasting color. Wildflowers would not be as vibrantly appealing if they were not scattered among sagebrush. The muted blue-green sage adds to the valley's color and certainly to the area's Old West flavor.

Nearly seventy percent of the park's forest is composed of lodgepole pine, a thin, tall ever-green tree. The Indians used this species for their lodges and tepees, hence the name lodgepole. Limber pine, the second-most common conifer, is found widely from the valley floor to treeline. This five-needle-to-a-bundle tree has a weathered and contorted profile when viewed from a distance. A very similar tree, often confused with limber pine, is whitebark pine. But whitebark pine usually is found only near treeline in the subalpine zone and is the rarest of the conifers. Yet, more so than any other conifer species, its myth and romanticism far exceeds its number.

The spire-like subalpine fir is soft to the touch when compared with Engelmann spruce. Both grow together in moist areas along streams and in mountain canyons.

In the fall—late September—deciduous trees stand in contrast to the dark evergreens. Cottonwoods and aspen turn to brilliant splashes of yellow and orange, distinct against the mountainsides.

The wildlife—flora and fauna—are abundant in the Tetons. They may not always be seen when you want. Be patient, nature has her own terms.

The diversity of habitats in Jackson Hole ranges from the nearly desert environment on the valley floor to a cold, subalpine environment on the mountain summits. Plants have adapted to these extremes and, as a result, the Tetons are rich in wildflowers.

Yellow buttercups, above, Yellowbells, lower left, and springbeauties, lower right, are some of the first flowers up in the spring. Shortly thereafter, balsamroot, center, and penstemons, right, cover the hillsides with their yellows and blues. Alpine forget-me-nots, upper center, and Parry's primrose, center right, withstand the harsh subalpine environment. Summer bloomers include sticky geranium, upper left, yellow pond lily, upper right, Indian paintbrush, center, left, and fireweed, lower center.

GEOLOGY

The Forces
That Shaped The Mountains

The Teton Range is an impressive group of peaks, rising abruptly nearly a vertical mile-and-a-half from the valley floor. The Grand Teton, at 13,770 feet, is the highest peak of the range and dominates the skyline. The range is nearly 40 miles long and 15 miles wide. But behind the facade of the mountains are the telltale clues that reveal their creation.

It has taken millions of years to create the Tetons. Like detectives, geologists have collected the bits and pieces of evidence that tell the Tetons' story. If we could go back 2.5 billion years and make a movie exposing one frame every 100 years, we would have a 434-hour-long film.

The first scene, 2.5 billion years ago (and still a billion years before the first traces of life) show rock formation in the womb of the Earth, ten miles below the surface. This rock would be moving and flowing like peanut butter from the pressure above and from heat below. Here, we would see the embryo of the Tetons for the first time. By the time this rock reaches the surface, it will be hard and durable, but that won't occur until the last 9 million years. The rock was formed by a process called metamorphism, meaning "to change." The rock changed to a layered gneiss (pronounced nice) composed of translucent quartz, opaque feldspar, black hornblende and flaky biotite (mica). While still below the surface, the gneisses were under great stress, which created cracks. These fractures were intruded by a molten rock that solidified into veins of light-colored pegmatite and dark-colored dikes of diabase. Upon close inspection, these light- and dark-colored veins are visible throughout the range. The east face of Mount Moran harbors a black wall about 150 feet thick near the summit. This is referred to as the black dike and is made of a hard durable diabase. Because it is harder

Glaciers are one of the greatest erosional forces and, during the past 15,000 years, have carved the peaks visible today. The Grand (left), Middle (center), and South (right) Tetons once had a ring of glaciers, like Schoolroom Glacier in the foreground, around them. These small glaciers are responsible for carving the peaks into sharp "Matterhorns."

Glaciers are moving streams of ice, fed by snowfall during winter. They represent the balance between the rate of accumulation and the rate of melting. If the climate warms, the glacier retreats, and when the climate cools, the glacier advances.

The moving stream of ice carries large quantities of rock-waste in the form of moraine from the higher valley slopes to the lower ones, at the same time wearing away the walls and hollowing out the floor. Like most other agents of erosion, glaciers carry out the threefold process of erosion, transportation and deposition.

Most of the transported morainic debris works its way to the edges or the front of a glacier, where it is deposited as a lateral or terminal moraine in the shape of a crescent, like Schoolroom Glacier at Hurricane Pass.

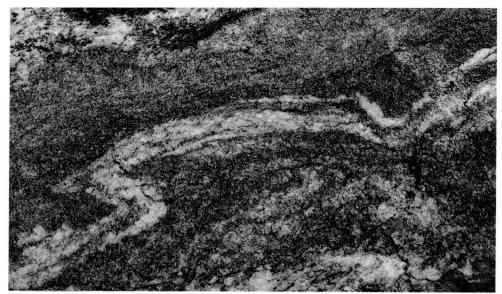

The Teton Range is comprised of folded bands of gneiss, a coarse textured metamorphic rock.

The block diagrams (facing page) are an oversimplification of the geologic process that has occurred during the past 2.5 billion years. The first diagram shows gneiss rock underlying sediments that were deposited by an ancient Paleozoic sea. Suddenly, 65 million years ago, the seas retreated and mountain uplifting began (2). Stresses deep within the earth began mountain building around the Teton country. As mountain-building stresses ceased, volcanic activity (3) began in the Yellowstone Absaroka area, depositing ash and debris in the Jackson Hole area. A large freshwater lake (4) formed after the volcanic period. Streams began eroding ash-covered mountains and depositing sediments in this large inland lake. Then, 9 million years ago, the Teton Range was forced upward (5) along a fracture called the Teton Fault. This fault caused the mountains to rise while Jackson Hole sank. Once the mountains were uplifted, other processes began shaping the range. Glaciers (6) are responsible for carving the mountains into sharp-pointed peaks and forming lakes at their bases during the past 15,000 years.

than the surrounding gneisses, it resists weathering, and thus stands out.

As the story continued for another 700 million years (121.5 hours of the movie) after the intrusion of the black dike, the gneiss rock slowly uplifted and eroded to a rolling plain. The scene changed when a large inland sea invaded most of the Intermountain West. For nearly 500 million years (87 movie hours), seas shifted like water in a plastic bag. During this important era, the rivers and streams laden with silt and sand flowed into the sea. The silt, sand, and skeletons of marine animals began to accumulate into thick sediment, tens of thousands of feet deep. This sediment still is present today on the very top of some of the Tetons, especially at the top of the aerial tram on Rendezvous Mountain, and on the east side of Jackson Hole in the Gros Ventre Mountains.

Suddenly, 65 million years ago, (11 hours before the movie ends), the seas retreated and mountain uplifting began. Mountains began forming in eastern Idaho and south of the Tetons. During the climax of the Laramide Revolution—5 million years or one movie hour—mountain building surrounded the Teton country. But at that time, the Tetons remained unformed, and not in the shape that we know them now.

When the excitement of the Laramide

Gravel, sand, and debris deposited by streams and glaciers (Quaternary).

Gray and white clay, limestone and volcanic ash deposited in lakes (Pliocene).

Brown conglomerate (Miocene and Upper Cretaceous).

Gray sandstone and slate (Upper Cretaceous).

Gray, green, red mottled sandstone, slate and limestone (Lower Cretaceous-Triassic).

Gray limestone, gray and green slate, and red brown sandstone (Paleozoic).

Gneiss, schist, and granite (Precambrian).

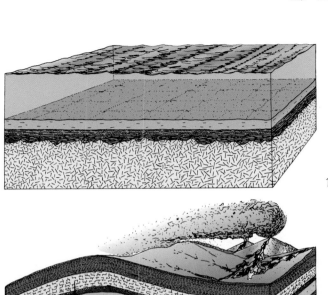

1.

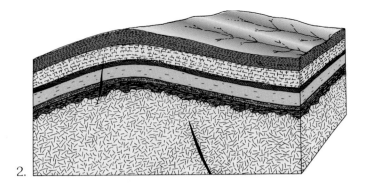

2.

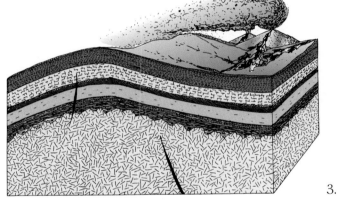

3.

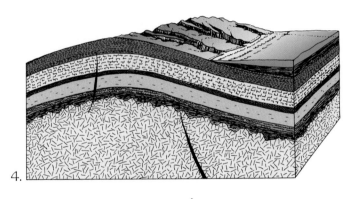

4.

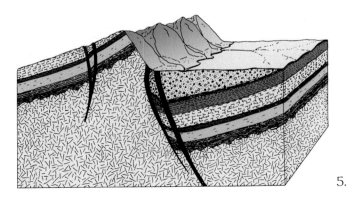

5.

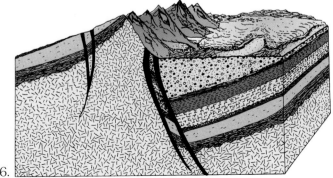

6.

Revolution subsided, volcanic activity began in the Yellowstone-Absaroka area, as volcanoes and calderas broke through the surface and erupted, leaving debris of ash and lava that filtered south into the valley. This continued sporadically for 20 million years (3.5 movie hours), as the northern region of Grand Teton National Park was covered with a blanket of volcanic ash and debris.

During the next 15 million years (2.5 movie hours), the Tetons underwent heavy erosion. Vast quantities of volcanic ash washed down into streams and were deposited in a freshwater lake called Teewinot Lake.

The last 9 million years (1.5 hours of the movie) were the climax. The Teton Range began to emerge and take form as it was pushed up. The formation of the range is a result of the Teton Fault, which runs along the base of the mountains. This fault caused two events: the uplift of the Teton range and the sinking of Jackson Hole. This displacement is more than 5.5 vertical miles. The fault is responsible for the abruptness of the mountains on their eastern

Evidence of glacial carving can be seen from the air, left, as glacial morainal lakes mark the entrance to canyons of the Teton Range. The shape of Cascade Canyon, above, right, is evidence of an ancient glacier traveling down a former stream valley, filling it with ice almost to the brim and changing its characteristic V form into a broad, steep-walled, U-shaped valley. Jenny Lake, at the end of Cascade Canyon, was formed by a terminal moraine after glaciers receded up the canyon.

side, where foothills are absent. But on the other side of the Tetons, there is no abrupt rise and the mountains gradually taper to the west. Erosion was responsible for cutting away the mountains as they rose. Erosion filled Jackson Hole with debris as the valley sank, leaving only about 1.5 miles of visible displacement.

As the mountain range rose, the underlying gneisses suddenly were exposed to erosion. The layered sediments also were lifted and formed a cap on top of the mountains. But because the limestones and dolomites are softer than the gneisses, they eroded faster.

Today, evidence of the ancient seas still are visible in Alaska Basin, on the summit of Mount Moran, and at the top of the aerial tram, where fossil corals, bivalves, and other ancient marine creatures can be found.

The concluding sequence began during the last 250,000 years (2.5 movie minutes), when the glacial age began. Glaciers were responsible for adding the finishing touches to the landscape. The last 250,000 years have brought three major glacial periods to the Tetons. The first was the largest and most widespread. The glacial ice flowed over Signal Mountain, Blacktail Butte, and the Gros

Ventre Buttes, carving them into boat-like shapes. The subsequent glacial periods were not as extensive. The second and last glaciation crisscrossed each of its predecessor's tracks. The third, the Pinedale Glaciation, created many of the features we see today. Jackson, Jenny, Leigh, Phelps, Bradley and Taggart lakes all are reminders of glaciers. The canyons originally were formed by streams, which cut them into V-shapes. When glaciers later flowed down the canyons, they broadened the canyons into wide U-shapes. Cascade Canyon exhibits this U-shaped glacier feature, and a hike up in the canyon reveals rock surfaces that were polished and grooved by the once-flowing ice. The sharp peaks themselves were cut into their distinct shapes by the frozen "rivers."

When the glaciers began to recede about 9,000 years ago (six seconds before the movie ends), man entered the scene, crossing the mountain passes in search of wild game and plants.

The abrupt rise of the west slope of the Tetons, left, is a result of the simplest structure produced by vertical movement—a block fault. This fault was caused by movement in opposite directions producing a fracture or crack, called the Teton Fault, in the rock. This mountain-building process began about 9 million years ago and continues even today.

The spire-like peak of the Grand Teton, right, and other sharp-pointed peaks were left as the last of the great ice ages receded nearly 15,000 years ago.

The film ends here. But we can make some predictions about the next unshot reel. The Tetons are a young mountain range and continue to grow as the valley sinks. In the past, this displacement has been along the Teton Fault at a rate of one foot in 100 years. This

will continue until an equilibrium is reached. Erosion then will overcome the lifting and eventually wear the mountains down to rolling hills. Meanwhile, to the north, Yellowstone Plateau remains dormant, with only geysers and thermal springs as residuals of its once-

powerful past, but it may resurrect itself and become volcanically active again.

✿ HISTORY ✿
Those Who Settled The Valley

The human history of Jackson Hole is short. Ancient civilizations flourished and died elsewhere before the first man stepped into this valley nearly 10,000 years ago. But in its own right, the story of Jackson Hole is just as intriguing as is the legacy of Rome or Athens.

The first people to visit this valley, shortly after the Pinedale Glaciation 12,000 to 15,000 years ago, wandered across the mountain passes on foot. Archaeological evidence found along the Snake River, passes, and along the shores of Jackson Lake indicate that these early visitors usually arrived in late spring, traveling in small bands across passes on the north and east entrances to

Early residents of Jackson Hole found summers magical and winters harsh and unforgiving. Ranchers soon discovered that "dudes" wintered better than cattle, and dude ranching became the way of life in Jackson Hole from the early turn of the twentieth century until recently. The Bar BC, left, was the second-oldest dude ranch in the valley and ran until the late 1980s. Now, however, it lays in ruins.

the valley. Thus, they probably left before the snow returned. They followed and used wild game, as those animals sought higher summer pastures. Primarily, they were seeking buffalo, elk, deer, and pronghorn—the main game that summered here. But early Native Americans did not subsist entirely on meat. Plants provided a greater portion of their food source during the summer months, and Jackson Hole provided an ample supply of berries, tubers, roots, and seeds.

The tribal names of the earliest people will remain unknown. It was not until the Spanish conquistadors introduced the horse to North America in about 1700 that Indians became mobile. With the European westward expansion, Indian tribes began shifting their territories, and new groups began spending summers in Jackson Hole.

The Crows, Blackfeet, Nez Perces (French for pierced nose, even though their noses were not pierced), Gros Ventre (French for big belly, even though they did not have big bellies), Shoshonis (or Snakes), and the Bannocks were in

this area until the 20th century. All of these tribes had horses, and with horses they no longer needed to follow wild game to the high mountain pastures. They then were able to travel greater distances, hunt and return to a home ground. Consequently, the Teton Valley no longer was an important summer range for migrating Indians.

The horse drastically changed the lives of the Indians. But in 1806 an event occurred along the Missouri River in Montana that altered the lives of the Indians of this area more severely.

In that year, the Lewis and Clark Expedition was on its return trip from the Pacific Ocean during its exploration of the Northwest. On their return journey, a young private and the expedition's hunter, John Colter, asked for his discharge to remain in the West to explore and hunt on his own. His discharge was granted, and he returned upriver to guide two trappers, Joseph Dickson and Forrest Hancock, whom he had just met working their way up the Missouri. He was outfitted with traps, tools, powder, lead and

The first explorers to Jackson Hole left little evidence of their visit. But John Colter, the first white man to visit Jackson Hole, reputedly is responsible for carving the "Colter Stone," lower left, in 1808. After Colter's arrival, other trappers and explorers discovered Jackson Hole's rich bounty of wild game, below. With the attraction of the mountains and the wild game, early residents, such as Katherine Yokel Brown, right, the first "lady dude wrangler," began dude ranching as a profitable business. Dude ranching, however, soon became too profitable, and the effects of uncontrolled exploitation began to show along the shores of Jenny Lake. John D. Rockefeller, Jr., left, was instrumental in purchasing valley land and donating it to the public for preservation. Today, the view of Jenny Lake, far right, is much the same as it was in the 1920s.

supplies enough to last two years. During that fall and winter, they trapped along the Yellowstone River and, for nearly a year, no one received news of him, until he was making his way alone in a dugout canoe that spring through the ice flow of the Yellowstone, heading for the Missouri and St. Louis. During Colter's sojourn, a wealthy St. Louis businessman named Manuel Lisa organized a company to retrace Lewis and Clark's footsteps. His intentions were to establish trading posts along the Missouri River and to encourage beaver-pelt trade with the Indians.

As Colter ventured down the Missouri River to St. Louis in his dugout in 1807, he met up with a keelboat carrying a large party of hunters and trappers led by Manual Lisa. Lisa then persuaded Colter to join his expedition and return to the wilderness once more, as their guide.

Lisa soon established a stockade on the Yellowstone River, near present-day Billings, Montana. This stockade became known as Manuel's Fort. One of Lisa's first orders was to send Colter, who had the most knowledge of Indians, on a goodwill expedition to encourage the

Cheyennes, Crows and Shoshonis to bring their pelts to the post for trade. Colter also was to explore the country to the south. In late November of 1807, the thirty-one-year-old Virginian, equipped with a thirty-pound pack, a flintlock rifle and some ammunition, set out on foot to explore the areas now known as Yellowstone and Grand Teton national parks.

Though literate, Colter never kept a diary of his journey, so his exact route will never be known. From a map drawn with Captain Clark years later, however, we are able to guess his route. He probably wandered into Jackson Hole from the Gros Ventre Mountains to the east. It would have been winter when he traveled on snowshoes across the valley, entering from the east and leaving across a pass south of the Teton Range. On the western slope of the Tetons, Colter must have made a temporary camp and, with his idle time, apparently carved a soft rhyolitic rock into the shape of a human head. On one side of the stone head are the deeply scratched letters: J O H N C O L T E R, and on the other side, the date: 1 8 0 8. The stone remained buried for more than a century, until 1931, when a father and son plowing their field in Teton Basin, Idaho unearthed it. Controversy has raged over the authenticity of this curious relic. Some call it a fake. The Colter Stone now is on display at the Park Service museum in Moose, and a replica is on display at the Jackson Hole Museum and Teton County Historical Society.

It was some time before other adventurous trappers began entering the valley in search of bea-

ver. Those who sought the valuable furs led a perilous and arduous life in the solitude of the mountains and without the companionship of women. The early French mountain men who trapped the beaver-rich streams on the western slopes of the Tetons soon began calling the prominent peaks Les

Trois Tetons—The Three Teats. The French version has persisted, even though the Grand Teton's name was changed to Mount Hayden in the early 1870s. Ferdinand Hayden, a government survey expedition leader, disapproved of that change. The name Grand Teton later was readopted.

Winters always were too harsh for the early trappers in the valley and most only traveled through here during summer. One trapper, however, did take up residence in Jackson Hole long enough to set his traps in the icy streams. David E. "Davey" Jackson had a fondness for this valley, and other trappers soon began calling the area "Jackson's Hole." The apostrophe "s" later was dropped. A hole is a valley surrounded by mountains, with no obvious way to escape. The name Jackson Hole is another reminder of our fur-trade era.

With the introduction of fashionable silk hats, beaver trapping became a dying business. By the 1840s, the Tetons once again became a place of solitude.

This calm lasted for more than 20 years before others ventured here. Just before the Civil War, government expeditions began exploring the Yellowstone and Grand Teton country to determine what use, if any, this country offered.

The first of the government expeditions was under the command of Captain William Raynolds. The legendary Jim Bridger acted as guide for the 1860 expedition. Bridger led the party down through the canyon of the Gros Ventre River into

Early settlers in Jackson Hole found winters rough and long, and the growing season short and unpredictable. After several discouraging years, homesteaders often would seek less harsh climates, abandoning their farms as this farmer did on Antelope Flats, left.

Right, a canoe excursion on String Lake during the 1920s brought as much excitement as it does today.

Jackson Hole and out over Teton Pass. After this, during the Civil War years, the valley was quiet for nearly another decade. Then the next major expedition, the Hayden Survey, occurred in 1872, lead into Jackson Hole by James Stevenson and guided by "Beaver Dick" Leigh.

The Hayden Survey named many of the lakes and peaks after its members. Frank Bradley and William Rush Taggart (Bradley and Taggart lakes), Joseph Leidy (Mount Leidy), Orestes St. John (Mount St. John), and Thomas Moran (Mount Moran), will always be remembered.

An ill-fated expedition in 1876 was led by Lt. Gustavus Doane. Doane was an ambitious man trying to gain fame as an explorer and leader. After several attempts to get endorsement to explore Africa, or appointment as superintendent of Yellowstone National Park, he finally was able to persuade his superiors to organize a small expedition down the Snake River. The boat trip started at the Snake's headwaters in Yellowstone and was to end at the Columbia River. For some

curious reason, Doane began his trip in winter. The group's supplies ran out. The men nearly starved because of the lack of game. Temperatures were below zero. They lost all of their equipment, and nearly their lives too, when their boat capsized in the Snake's icy waters. At that point, 68 days

and a disappointing 200 miles from the start, Doane wanted to retrace his route to rewrite his lost journals. To the relief of his emaciated men, Doane's superiors sent a telegram ordering the end of the expedition.

The government surveyors ushered the way for those seeking gold and land. The prospectors, having left the gold fields of Montana and California, began seeking their fortunes here. There has never been abundant gold in Jackson Hole. At first, though, expectations were high.

In the spring of 1886, four German men built a gold sluice and a small cabin on a Snake River sand bar, just below Snake River Overlook. Their gold returns were meager, and eventually, tension developed among the four men. Later that summer, a party of fishermen discovered three bodies in the river, weighted down by rocks. The fishermen sought help and reported the apparent murders to authorities in the valley. They immediately suspected the missing fourth member of the group, a man named Tonnar. A posse found him working on a nearby hay ranch. He then admitted killing the three men, but claimed self-defense, stating that his partners had beaten him for his claim. Subsequently, a violent quarrel broke out and the killings followed. During the trial, the prosecution offered only circumstantial evidence, and Tonnar was found innocent. Upon his release, he left the area immediately. Today, just below Snake River Overlook, on the Rockefeller Parkway road, the ill-fated prospectors' sand bar and remnants of their small cabin, remain. It now bears the appropriate name of Deadman's Bar.

The government surveyors ushered in another group—the homesteaders. They were a rugged people who came to build homes, break the sod for cultivation, and raise livestock. It was

Menor's Ferry, left, one of the few remaining historic sites in the valley, has a setting of the 1900s. The restored cabin and interior of Bill Menor's old home and store testifies to a life of hard work and simple conveniences. The ferry, located a mile north of Moose, is open to the public.

a hard living, marked by cold, long winters, isolation and loneliness. The first settlers usually were bachelors, but soon Mormon families began arriving and the population grew rapidly. By 1897, the town of Jackson was founded. It consisted of only a few buildings.

In 1892, one homesteader decided there was a need to cross the Snake River without getting wet feet. Bill Menor built his ferry to shuttle people and their livestock from one side to the other. The ferry was in operation until 1927, when a bridge was built. Menor's Ferry, located north of Moose, is one of the few historic sites left in the valley, and it occasionally is open to the public.

As the population of Jackson Hole grew, official justice did not always keep up, but vigilante law did. When necessary, citizens took matters into their own hands. This often is portrayed in the Wild West when dealing with rustlers.

In an 1892 incident, referred to as "the Cunningham Cabin Affair," two horse thieves brought their stolen animals to Jackson Hole for the winter to allow the new brands to heal. They bought hay from Pierce Cunningham, a rancher, who allowed them to use his northern summer cabin for the winter. Rumors soon reached Montana that there were thieves here harboring horses stolen from that state. By the spring of 1893, two men snowshoed over Teton Pass and, saying they were lawmen from Montana, collected a posse. On April 15, seven men, forming the posse, waited on a bluff overlooking the

cabin until dawn, when the men emerged. Though the posse shouted to the outlaws to throw down their weapons, the horse thieves began firing. The posse returned fire and the two men were killed.

After the shootout, the posse wrapped the

bodies in blankets and buried them in an unmarked grave, keeping the incident a secret. Years later, however, the story surfaced. An investigation never determined if the two "lawmen" from Montana were officials. But this was Western justice.

It did not take ranchers and farmers long to discover that cold, harsh winters and short, cool summers were not the best environment for rais-

ing cattle and crops. They soon discovered that it was more profitable to "raise" tourists instead. By the turn of the century, the first dudes relished in the delight of fishing, hunting, and relaxing under the spell of the Grand Tetons. The valley and mountains soon became a place to cherish, and some realized that the Tetons needed protection from encroaching commercialism. In 1918, Congress attempted to extend Yellowstone Park's boundary to include the Tetons. This proposal failed because sheep ranchers believed the plan would prevent them from grazing their sheep on the western slope of the Tetons. Though this initial action to protect the Tetons died, the conservation spirit and fight continued.

When Horace Albright became superintendent of Yellowstone National Park in 1919, mixed emotions continued to rage over the establishment of a national park for the Tetons. Albright discovered that conventional means of protecting the Teton landscape would not work. So, in 1926, when John D. Rockefeller, Jr. visited Yellowstone, Albright brought him down to the Tetons for Rockefeller's first visit. Immediately impressed by the grandeur of the mountains, Rockefeller believed they should be protected and the valley floor preserved.

Dude-ranch life in the valley provided idyllic and carefree days for "dudes," who spent their summers here escaping the heat and jobs of their Eastern cities.

He quietly returned to New York and later asked Albright to draw a map and estimate the cost of private land in the valley. By 1927, Rockefeller formed the Snake River Land Company, a front to keep landowners from asking exorbitant sums from the millionaire. By 1930, the company owned most of the private land on the valley floor. It soon leaked, however, that Rockefeller was behind the purchase, and public dissent followed. Some believed that Rockefeller was trying to cheat landowners by underhanded methods. A Senate subcommittee found that Rockefeller had been fair in all of his dealings and had given generous prices for the land.

In 1929, Congress decided to establish Grand Teton National Park from national forest lands. The original park, however, protected only the peaks and did not include all of the lakes at their bases. By 1943, after years of unsuccessful attempts to donate his land to the national park, Rockefeller made a decree. Either the land was to be accepted as a gift to the public or it would be sold.

The threat immediately prompted President Franklin Roosevelt to use executive authority to create the Jackson Hole National Monument out of public lands, mainly national forests, but Rockefeller's threat did not carry much weight because the land was not officially accepted until 1949. The boundaries also encompassed private lands, including the Rockefeller property. This action caused considerable debate, both locally and in Washington. Congress believed only it had the authority to create national parks and it did not like the interference of the president settling its disputes. To show its resentment, Congress submitted a bill to abolish the president's national monument, but Roosevelt killed the bill with a pocket veto. For seven years, skirmishes continued until Congress, in 1950, passed a bill to incorporate the national monument as part of what now is the national park.

These were the people who settled the valley. The first came to seek game and berries, to trap beaver, to explore, to seek gold, and to homestead and ranch. They were hardy people who often sought solitude rather than the comforts of city life, but they all had one common love ... the love of the mountains.

Most of the traditional ranches are gone today, but their legacy lives on.

BIBLIOGRAPHY

HIKING AND GENERAL

Bonney, Lorraine G. 1995. *Bonney's Guide to Jackson's Hole and Grand Teton National Parks.* Moose, Wyoming: Homestead Publishing.

Editors of Homestead Publishing. 1997. Grand Teton Hiking Map. Moose, Wyoming: Homestead Publishing.

Lawrence, Paul. 1973, *Hiking the Teton Backcountry.* San Francisco: Sierra Club.

Schreier, Carl. 1997. *Hiking Jackson Hole Trails.* Moose, Wyoming: Homestead Publishing.

Turiano, Thomas. 1995. *Teton Skiing.* Moose, Wyoming: Homestead Publishing.

NATURE

Carrighar, Sally. 1967. *One Day at Teton Marsh.* New York: Alfred A. Knopf.

Murie, Margaret and Olaus. 1969. *Wapiti Wilderness.* New York: Alfred A. Knopf.

Perry, William, and editors of Homestead Publishing. 1995. *Rocky Mountain Wildlife of Yellowstone and Grand Teton National Parks.* Moose, Wyoming: Homestead Publishing.

Raynes, Bert. 1995. *Birds of Jackson Hole.* Moose, Wyoming: Homestead Publishing.

Raynes, Bert. 1995. *Wildlife of Yellowstone & Jackson Hole.* Moose, Wyoming: Homestead Publishing.

Schreier, Carl. 1996. *A Field Guide to Wildflowers of the Rocky Mountains.* Moose, Wyoming: Homestead Publishing.

Shaw, Richard J. 1974 and 1981. *Plants of Yellowstone and Grand Teton National Parks.* Salt Lake City, Utah: Wheelright Press.

GEOLOGY

Love, J.D., and Reed, John C. Jr. 1968. *Creation of the Teton Landscape.* Moose, Wyoming: Grand Teton Natural History Association.

Schreier, Carl. 1992. (2nd ed) *A Field Guide to Yellowstone's Geysers, Hot Springs and Fumaroles.* Moose, Wyoming: Homestead Publishing.

HISTORY

Betts, Robert B. 1978. *Along the Ramparts of the Tetons.* Boulder, Colorado: Colorado Associated University Press.

Clary, David A. 1993. *The Place Where Hell Bubbled Up.* Moose, Wyoming: Homestead Publishing.

Sanborn, Margaret. 1993. *The Grand Tetons: The Story of Taming the Western Wilderness.* Moose, Wyoming: Homestead Publishing.

EDUCATIONAL OPPORTUNITIES

Since 1988, the Snake River Institute has used the West as its classroom. The Institute, a nonprofit educational institution, offers exciting subject matters in science, archaeology, Western history, art, writing and culture. The Snake River Institute provides courses running between one- and five-day summer seminars taught by experienced instructors to study a wide range of natural-history topics, including geology, wildflowers, animal behavior and photography. The courses are held primarily between May and November and are for learners of all ages.

For more information or a catalog, please contact:
The Snake River Institute
P.O. Box 128
Wilson, Wyoming 83014
(307) 733-2214

SERVICES

FLAGG RANCH VILLAGE - campground (private), trailer village, accommodations, service station, snack bar, restaurant, grocery store, bar and lounge, gift store, horse rides.
LIZARD CREEK - campground (Park Service).
LEEK'S MARINA - restaurant, marina, boat gas, tackle shop.
COLTER BAY - campground (Park Service),

visitor center, trailer village (with hookups), service stations, cabins, restaurant, snack bar, grocery store, convenience store, marina, gift store, bicycle rentals, horse rides, showers, laundry, firewood, ATM.
JACKSON LAKE LODGE - cabins, service station, restaurant, bar and lounge, gift shops, horse rides, swimming pool, beauty shop, ATM.
SIGNAL MOUNTAIN - campground (Park Service), cabins, service station, convenience store, restaurant, grocery store, bar and lounge, marina, gift shop.

MORAN - post office.
TRIANGLE X RANCH - dude ranch facilities.
JENNY LAKE - campground (Park Service), groceries, boat shuttle service, climbing guide service, gifts, bicycle rentals (at Jenny Lake Lodge — cabins, dining room).
MOOSE - visitor center, housekeeping cabins, service station, snack bars, chuckwagon, bar and lounge, canoe rentals, outdoor-equipment stores, bicycle shop, gift store, post office, ATM.
KELLY/GROS VENTRE - campground (Park Service), post office.

OUTSIDE GRAND TETON NATIONAL PARK AT JACKSON AND TETON VILLAGE - All services available, including a hospital in Jackson and a medical clinic in Teton Village.

OTHER BOOKS IN THIS SERIES
Grand Teton
Yellowstone
Glacier-Waterton
Banff-Jasper

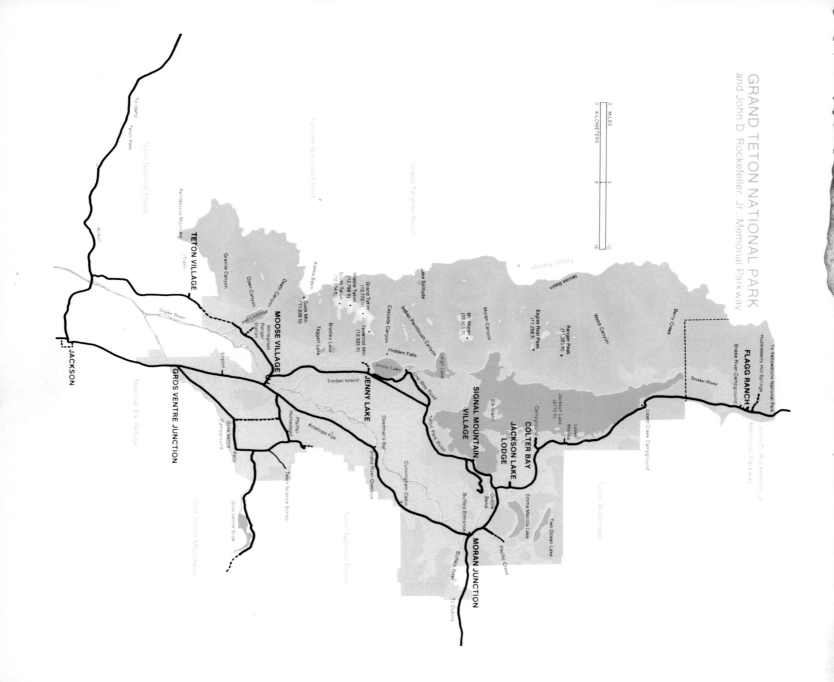

GRAND TETON NATIONAL PARK
and John D. Rockefeller, Jr. Memorial Parkway

MILES
KILOMETERS
0
0
5
8
10
16

To Idaho

Teton Pass

Teton National Forest

Rendezvous Mountain
(Tram)

Targhee National Forest

Grand Targhee Resort

Teton Range

TETON VILLAGE

Granite Canyon

Open Canyon

Death Canyon

Alaska Basin

Buck Mtn.
(11,938 ft)

Moose Basin

Wister

Snake River

JACKSON

Whitegrass
Ranger
Station

Phelps Lake

MOOSE VILLAGE

Grand Teton
(13,770 ft)
Middle Teton
(12,798 ft)
South Teton
(12,514 ft)
Teewinot Mtn.
(12,325 ft)

Bradley Lake

Taggart Lake

Cascade Canyon

Lake Solitude

Indian Paintbrush Canyon

Mt. Moran
(12,605 ft)

Moran Canyon

Eagles Rest Peak
(11,258 ft)

Ranger Peak
(7,365 ft)

Webb Canyon

Berry Creek

Snake River

FLAGG RANCH

Huckleberry Hot Springs
Snake River Campground

To Yellowstone National Park

John D. Rockefeller, Jr. Memorial Parkway

GROS VENTRE JUNCTION

National Elk Refuge

Airport

Homestead
Pfeiffer

Antelope Flat

Deadman's Bar

Timber Island

Hidden Falls

Jenny Lake

JENNY LAKE

Leigh Lake

One Way Road

String Lake

Elk Island

Teton Park Road

SIGNAL MOUNTAIN
VILLAGE

Jackson Lake
(6770 ft)

Leeks
Marina

COLTER BAY

JACKSON LAKE
LODGE

Campground

Lizard Creek Campground

Teton Wilderness

Gros Ventre

Campground

Kelly

Teton Science School

Cunningham Cabin

Snake River Overlook

Cascade Canyon

Cathedral
Bend

Buffalo Entrance

Pacific Creek

Emma Matilda Lake

Two Ocean Lake

Snake River

Gros Ventre Mountains

Gros Ventre Slide

Teton National Forest

Buffalo River

MORAN JUNCTION

To Dubois